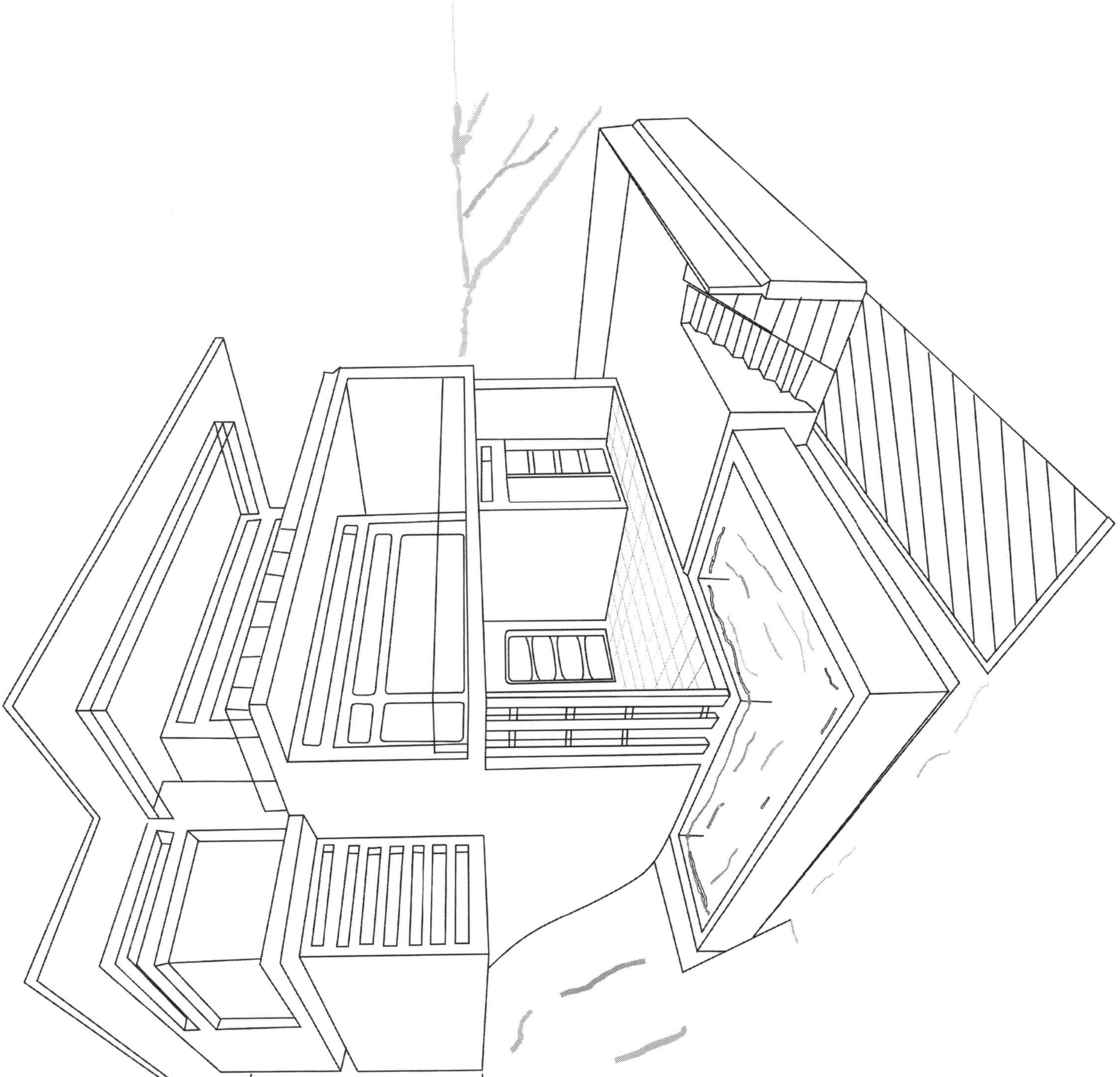

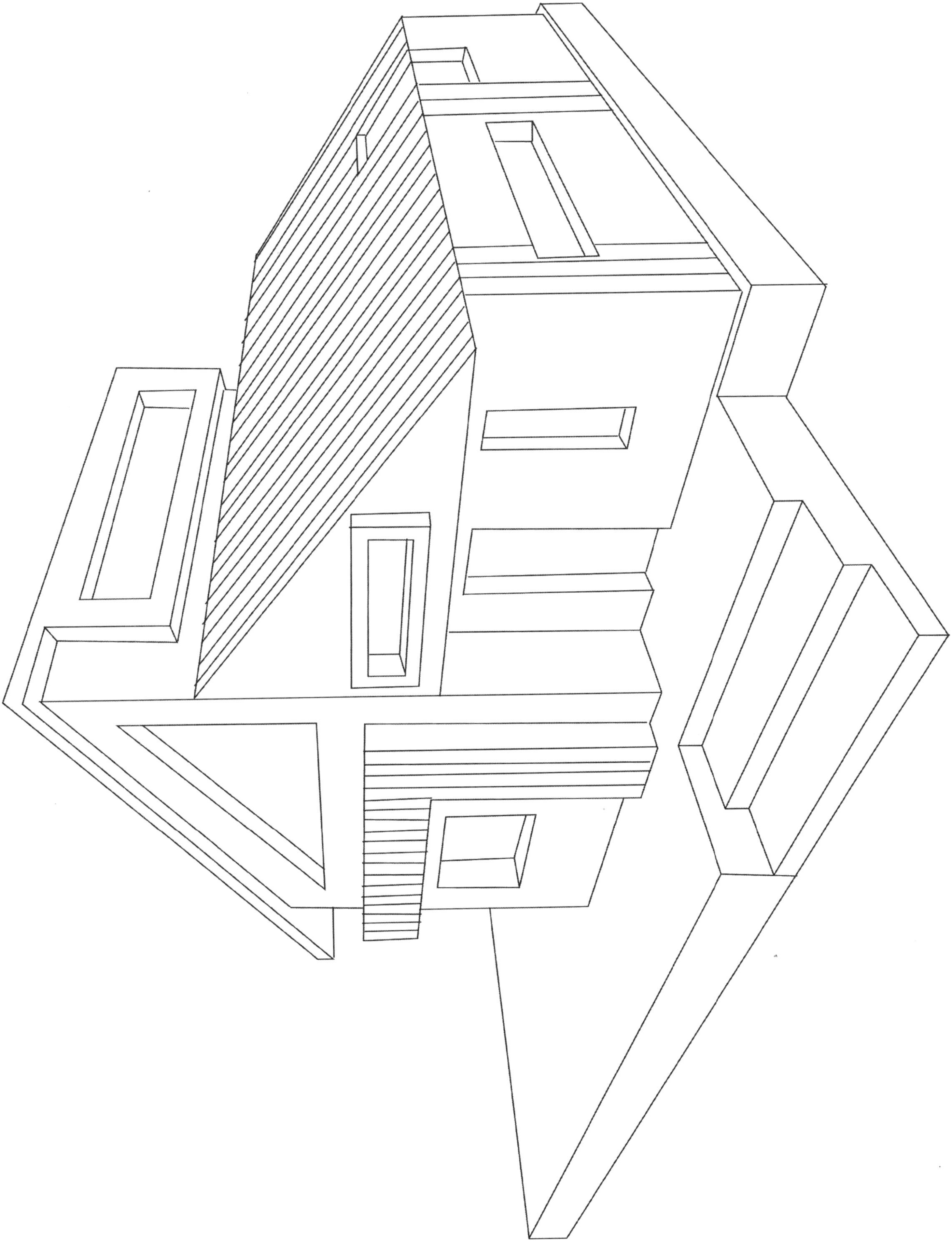

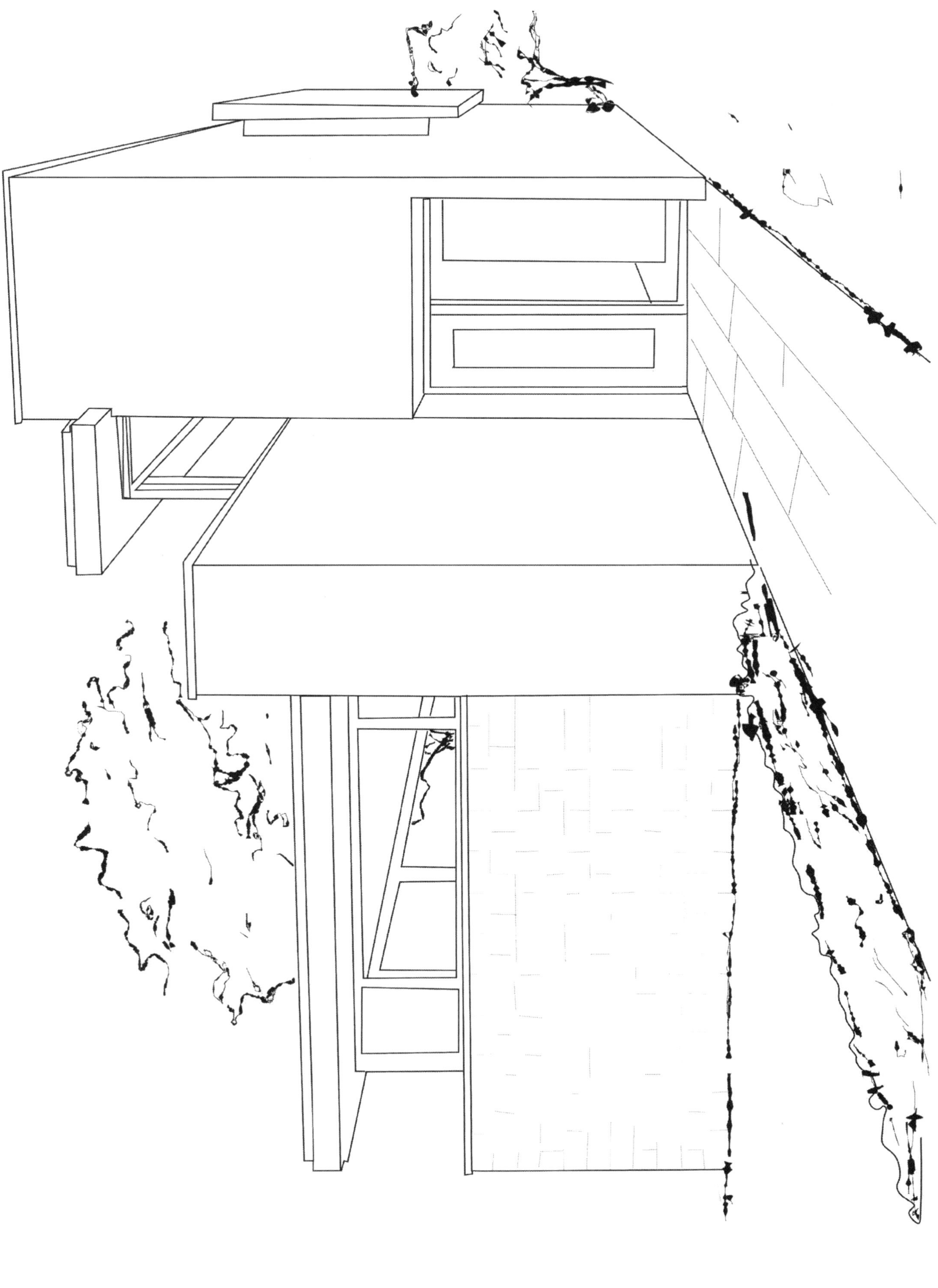

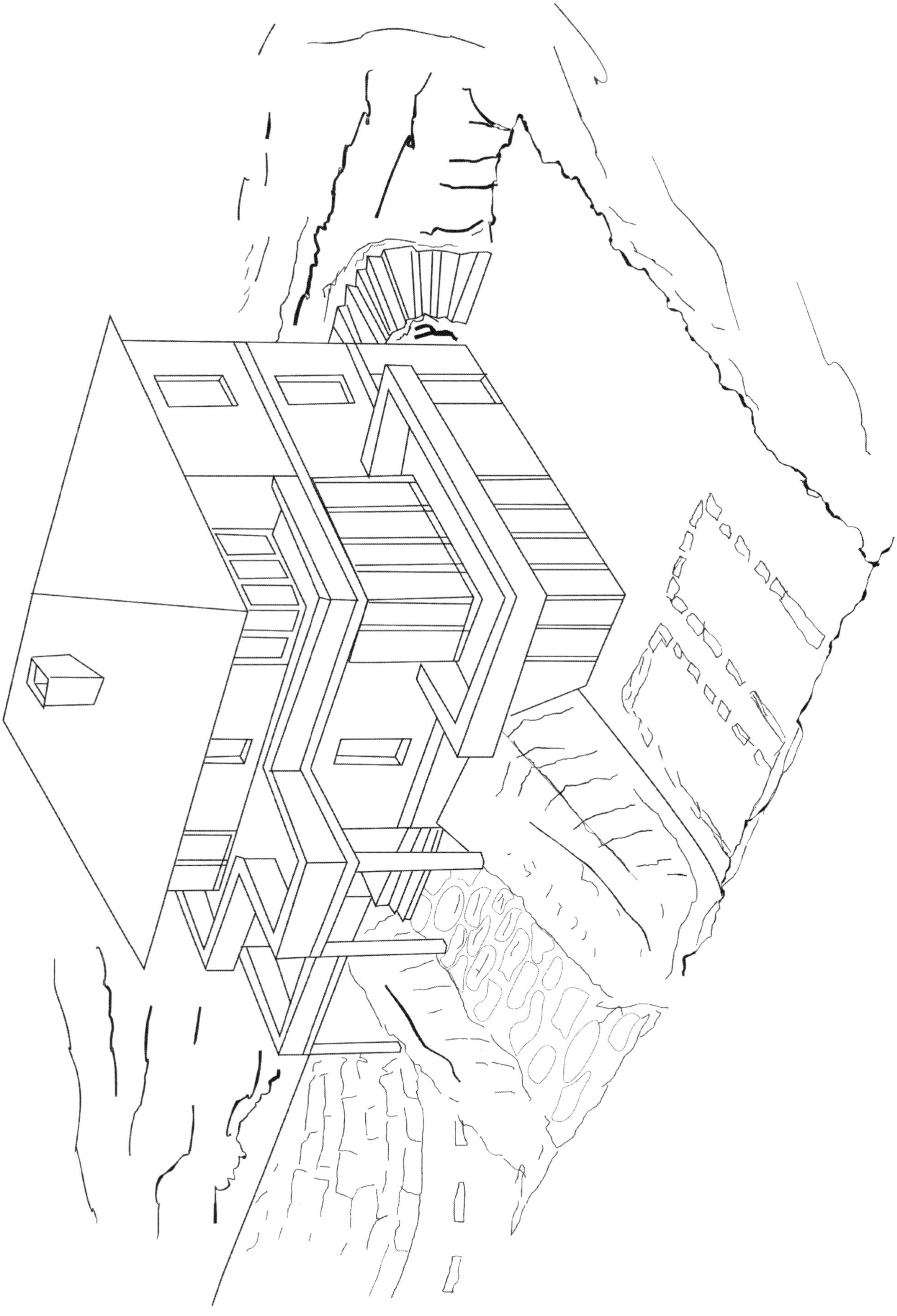

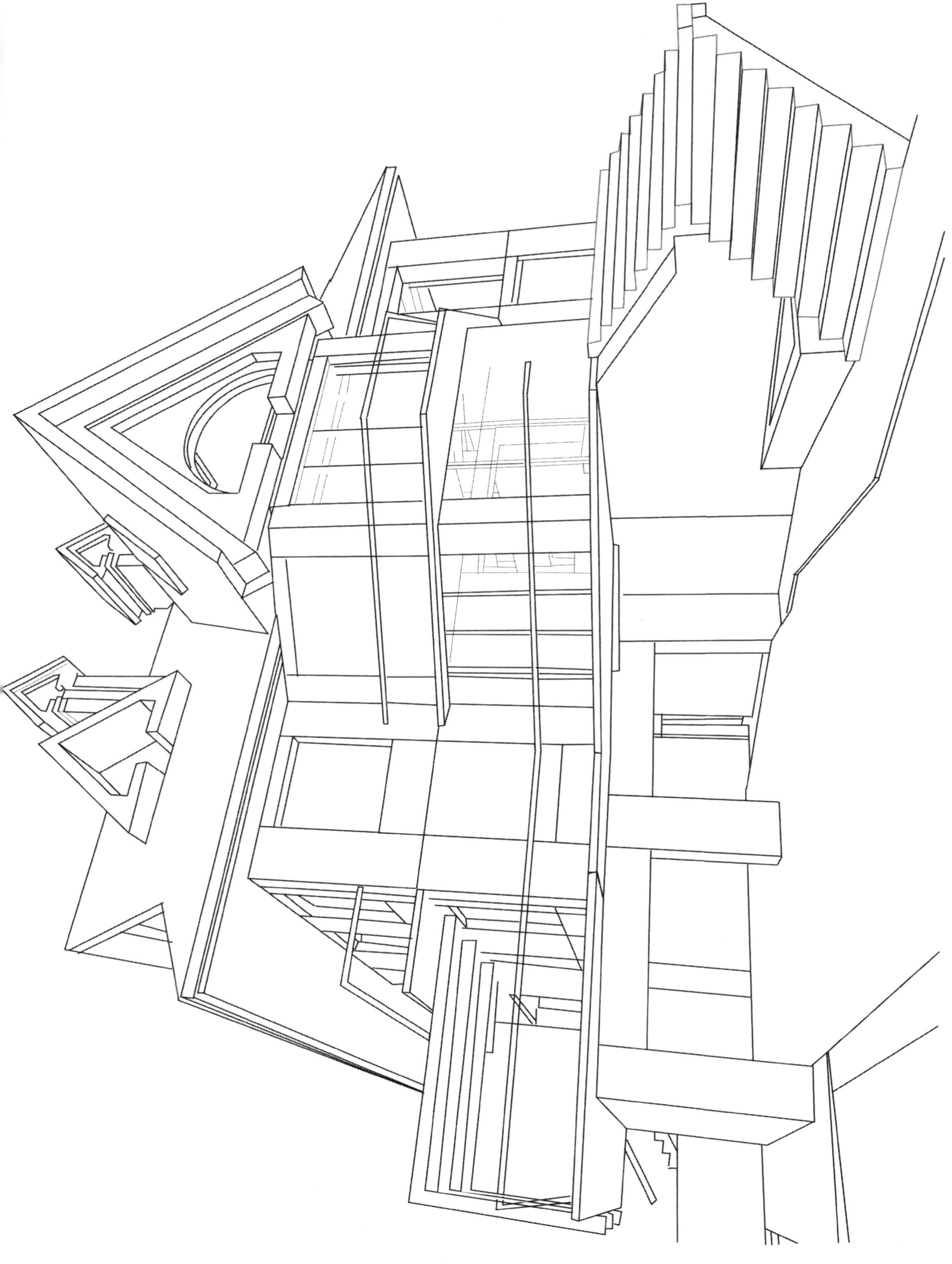

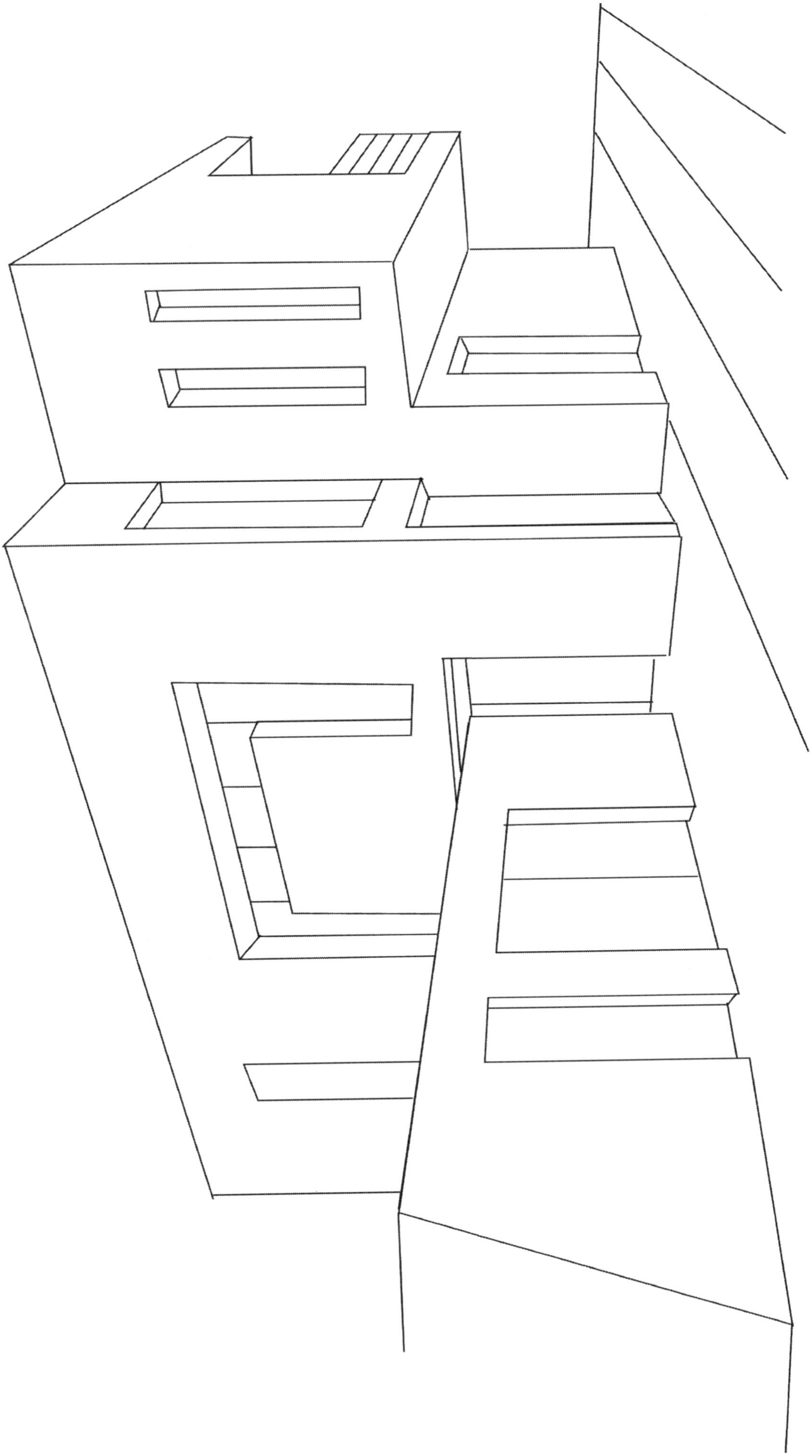

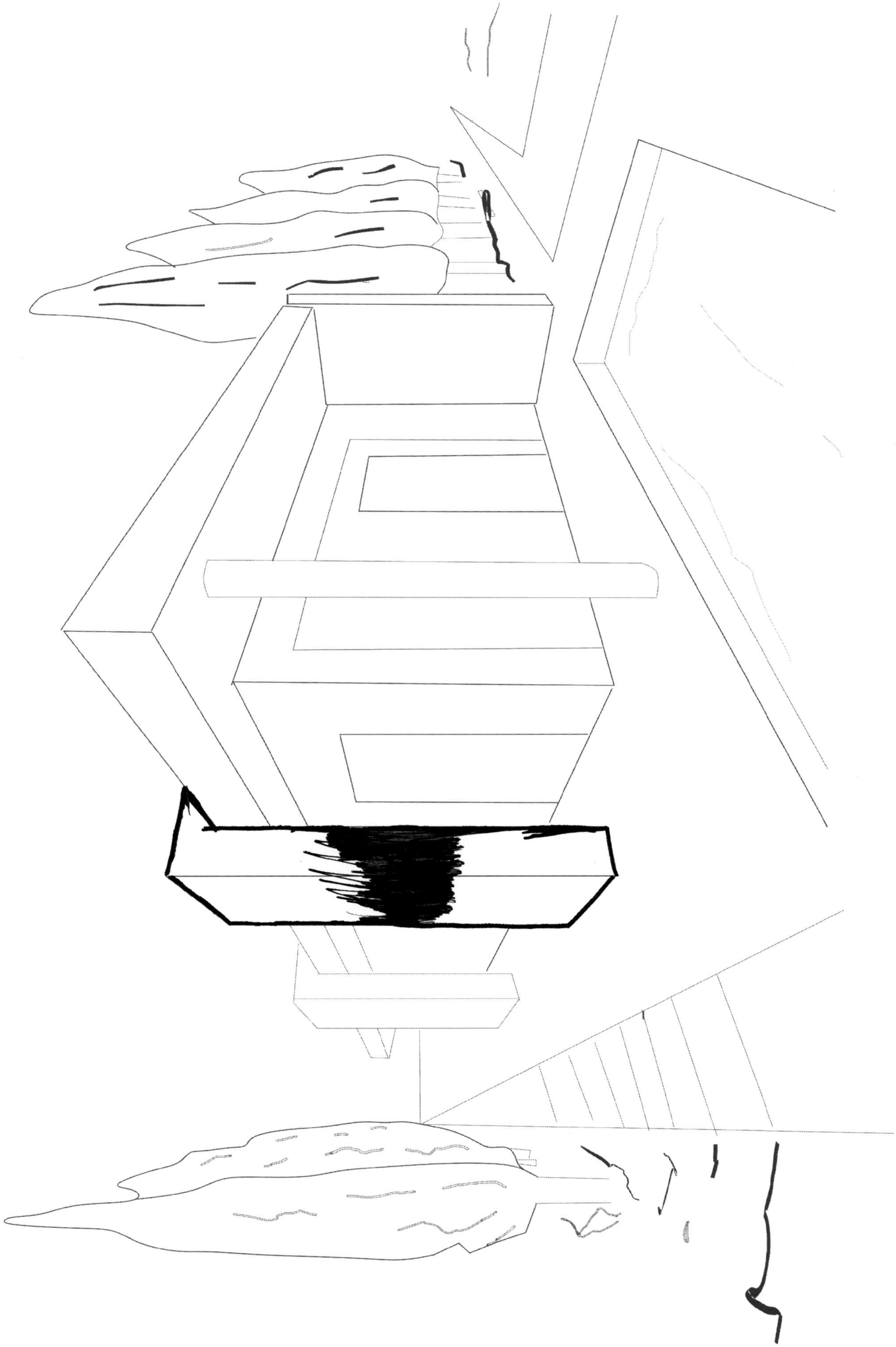

BOUTIQUE
TOYS
BOOK STORE
CLOSED
CLOSED
CLOSED

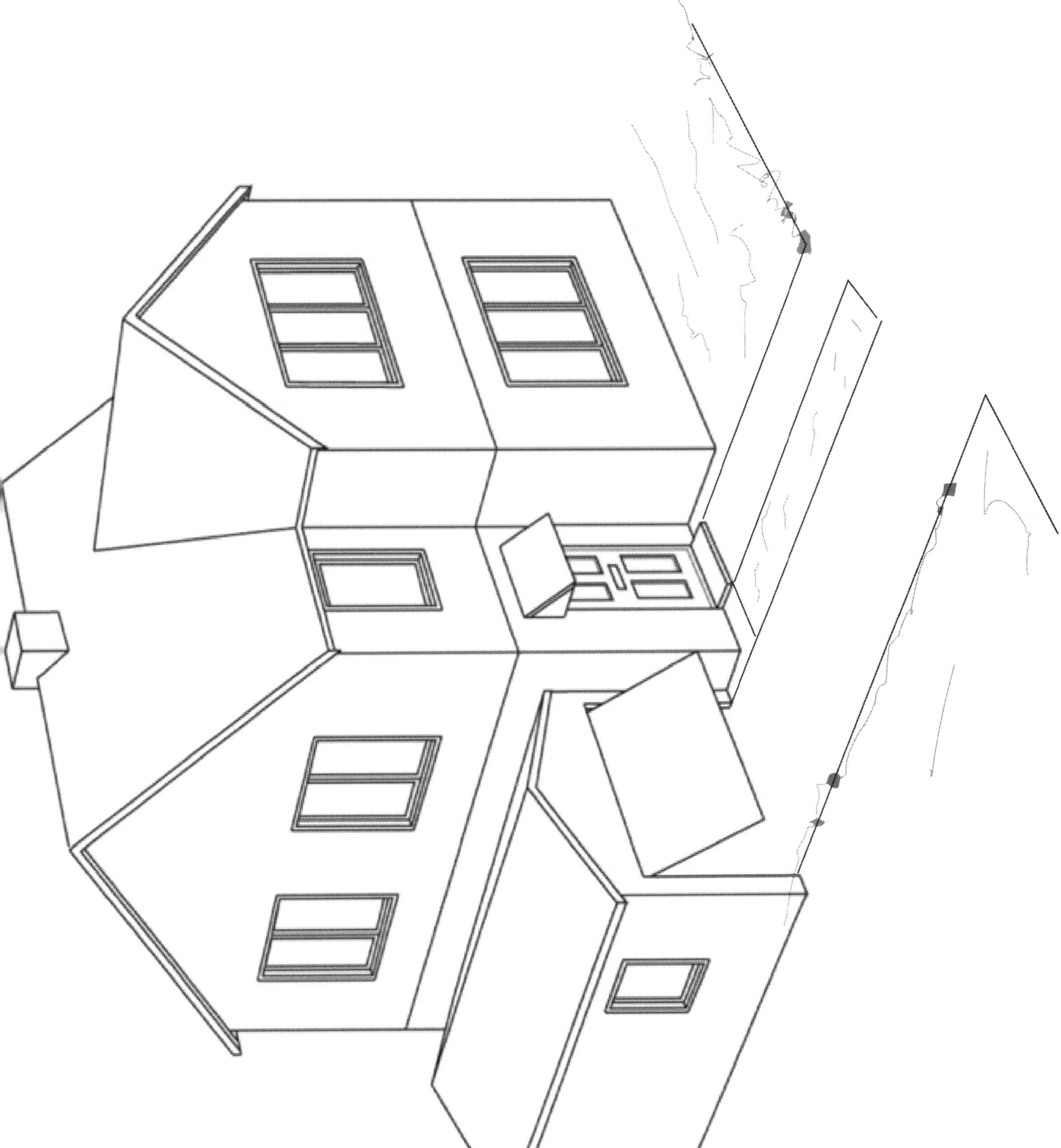

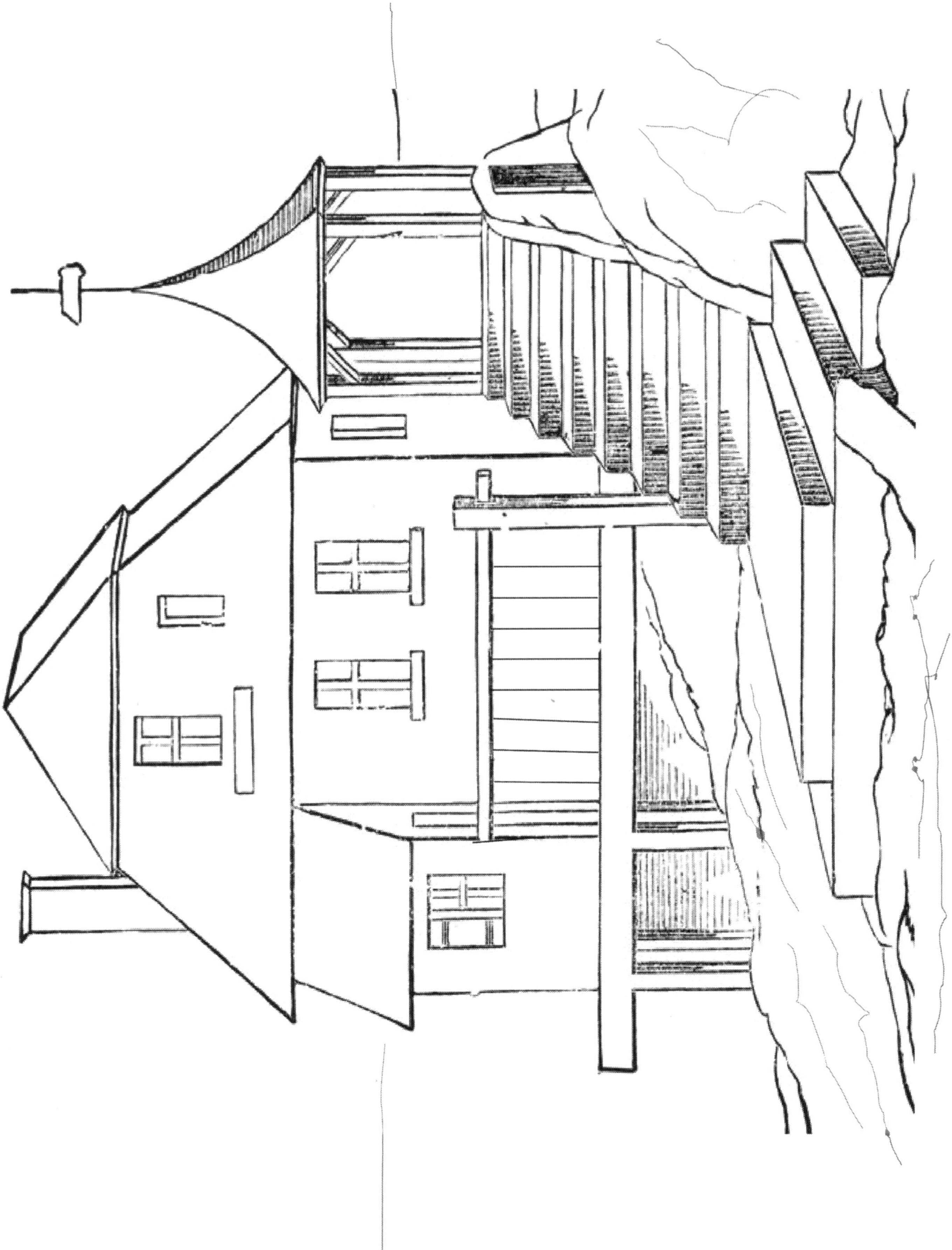

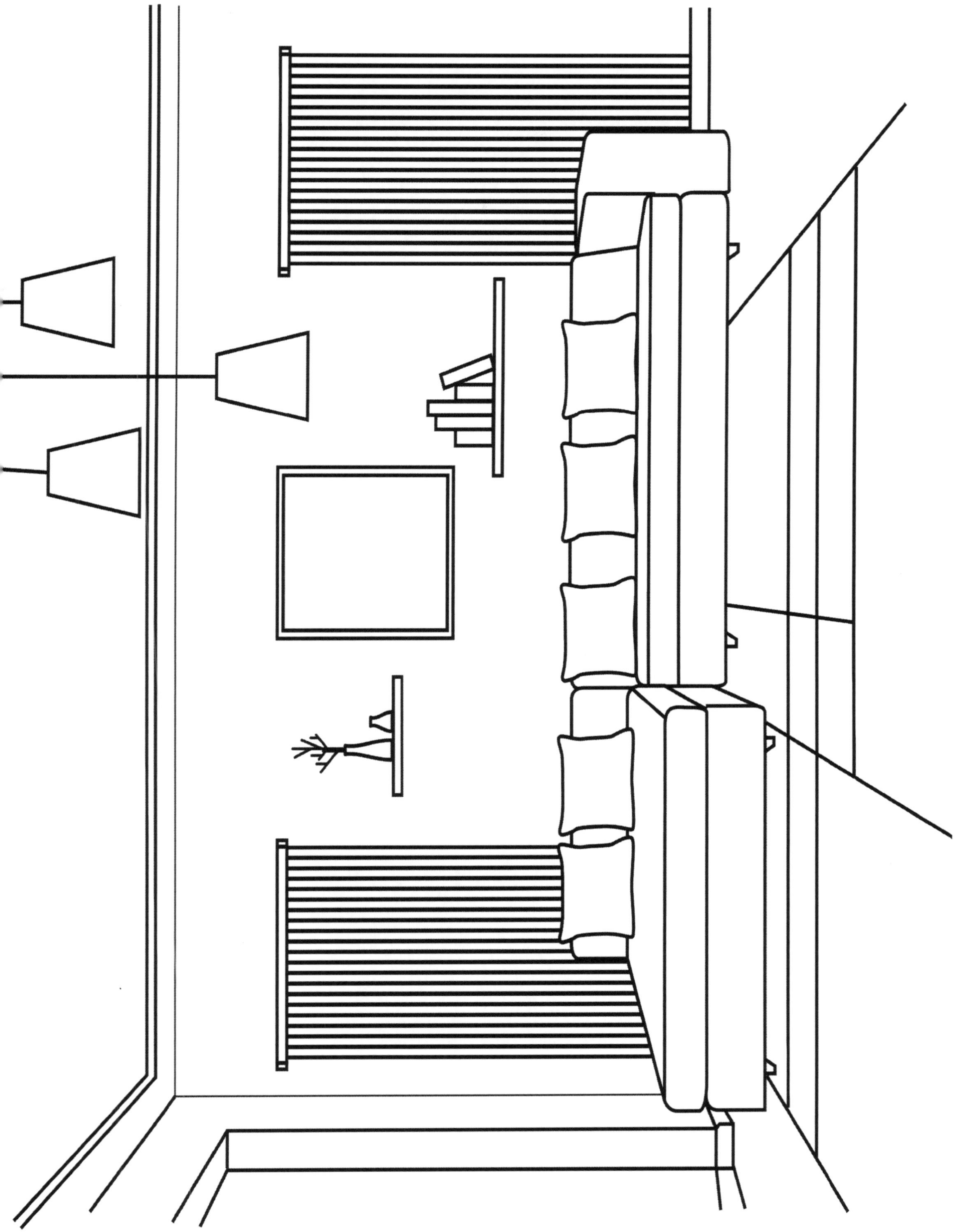

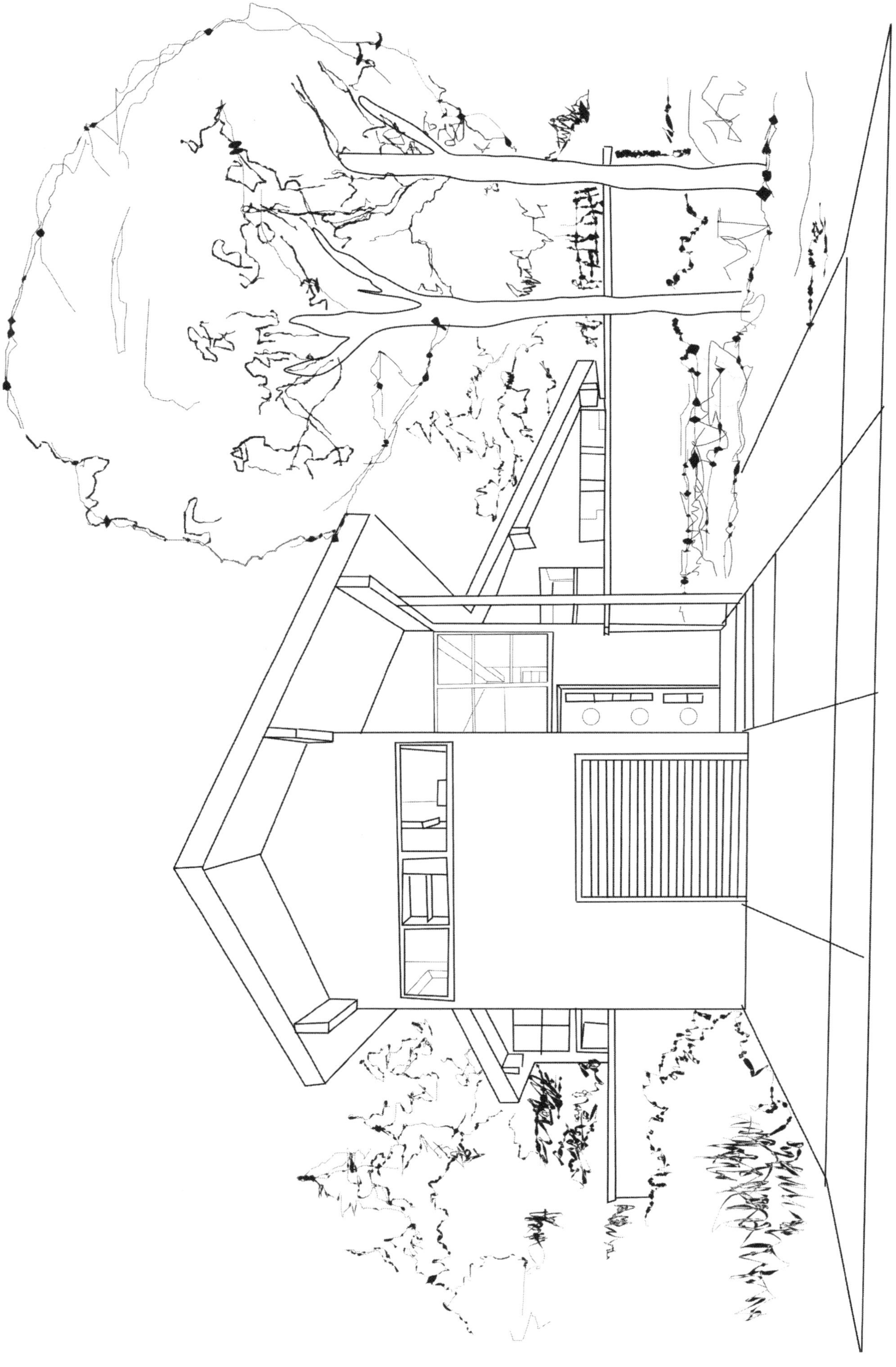

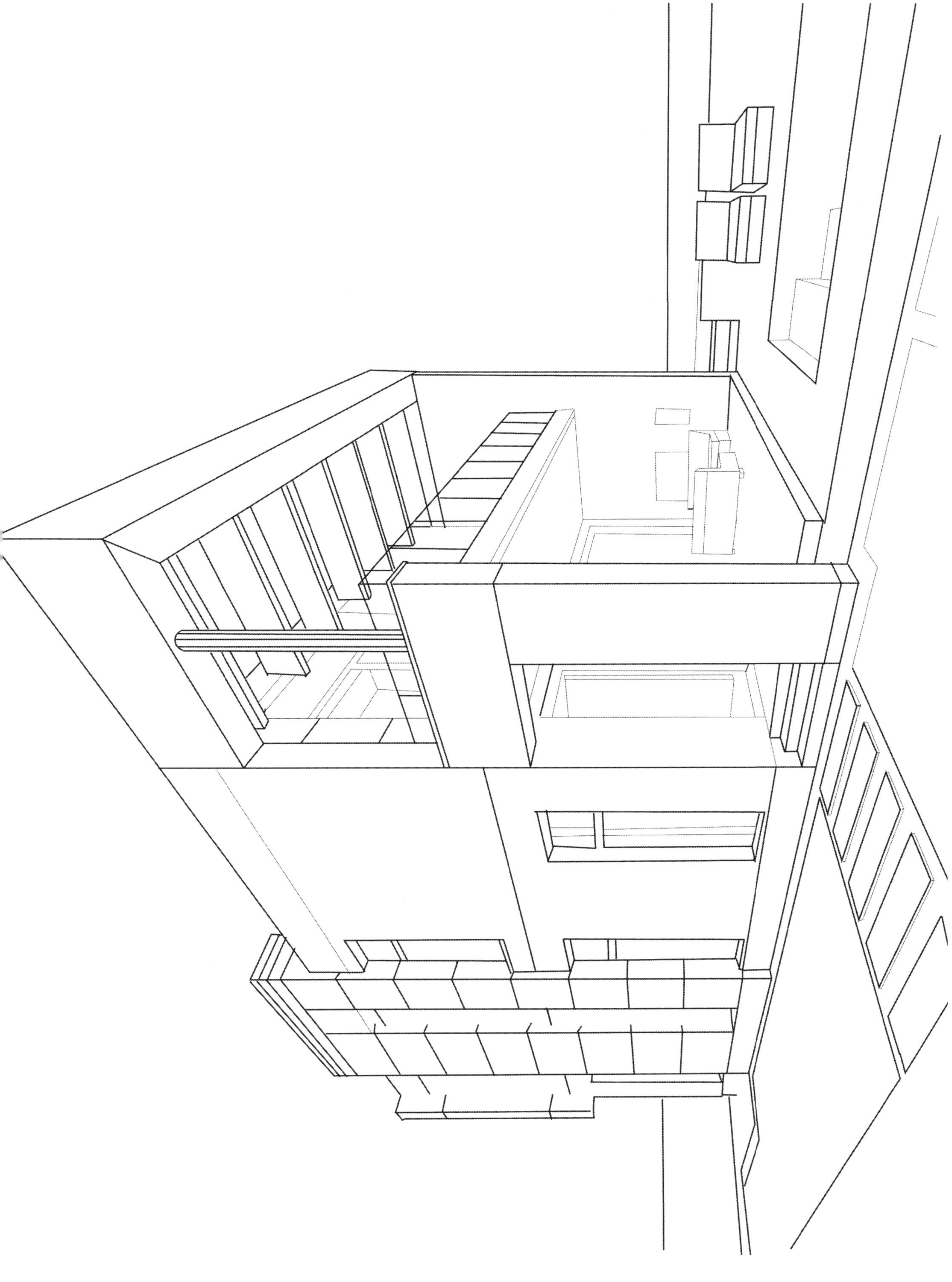

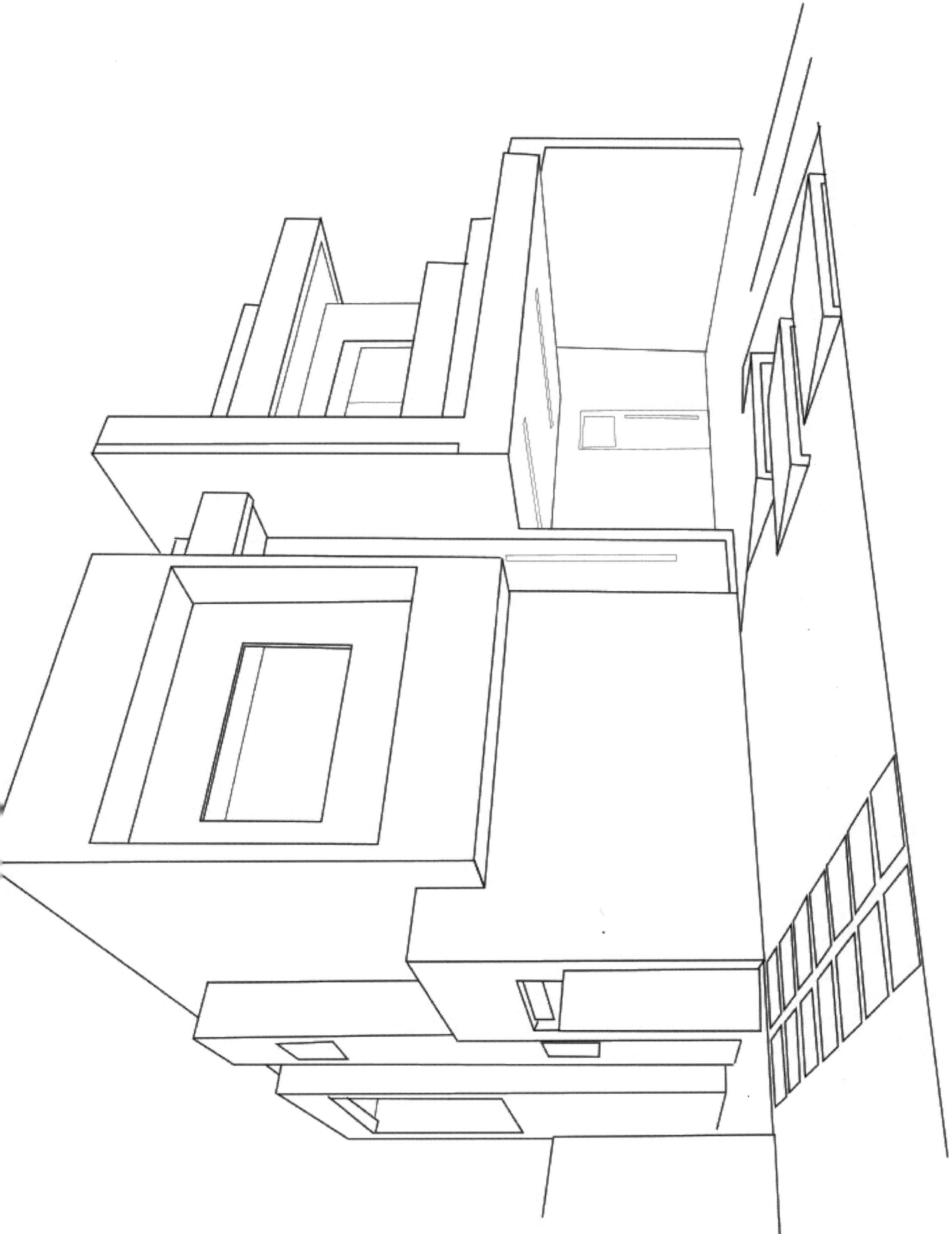

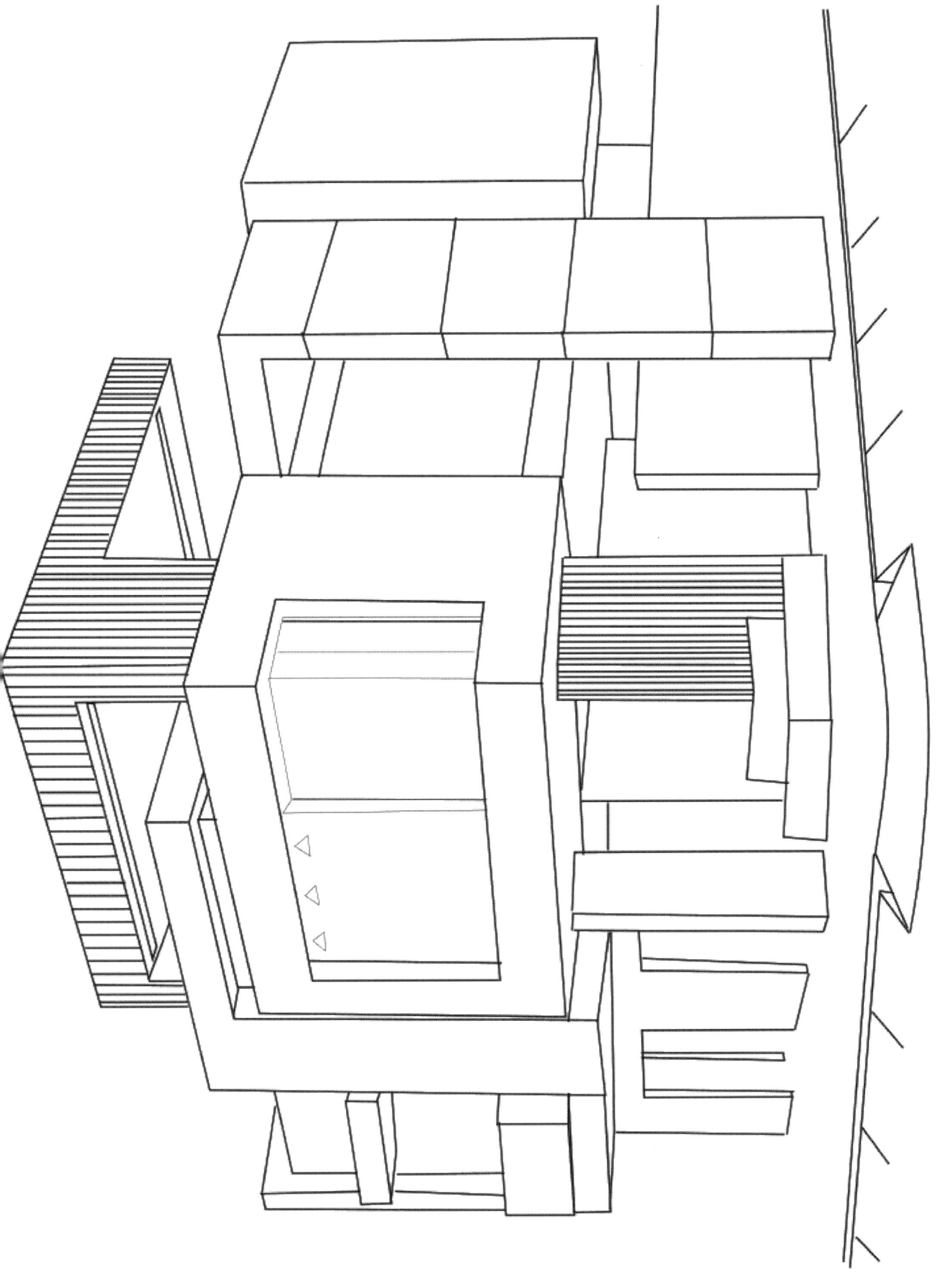

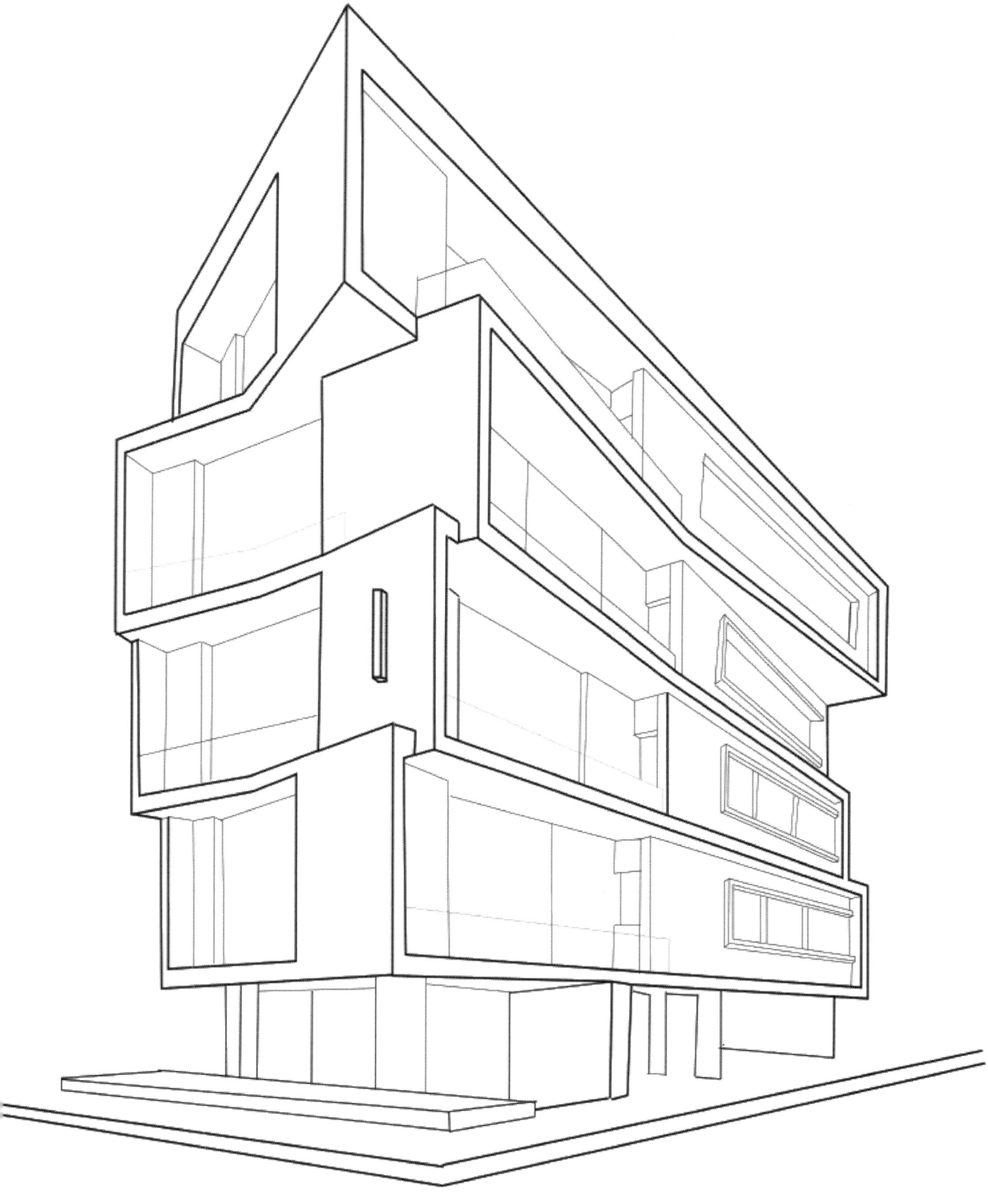

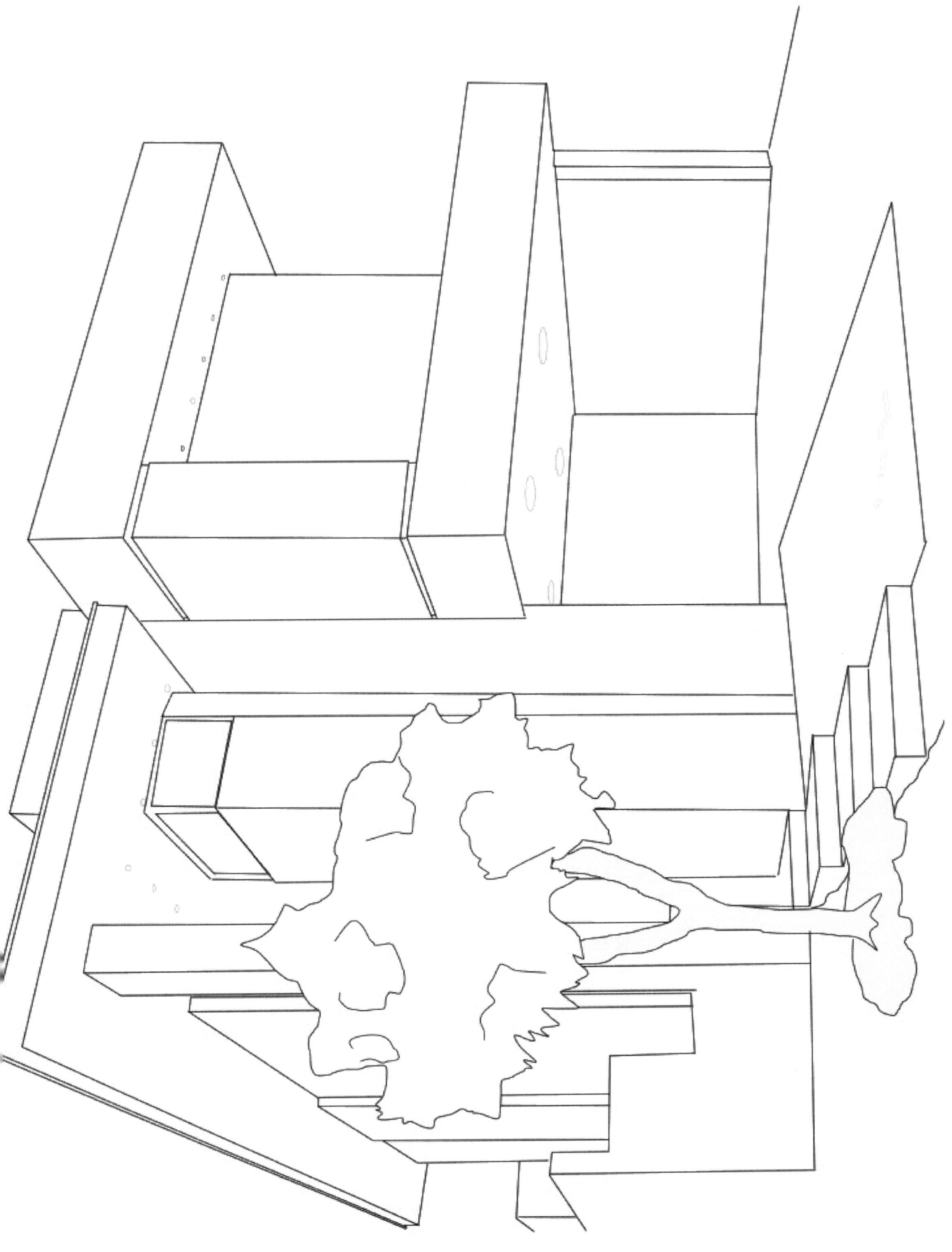

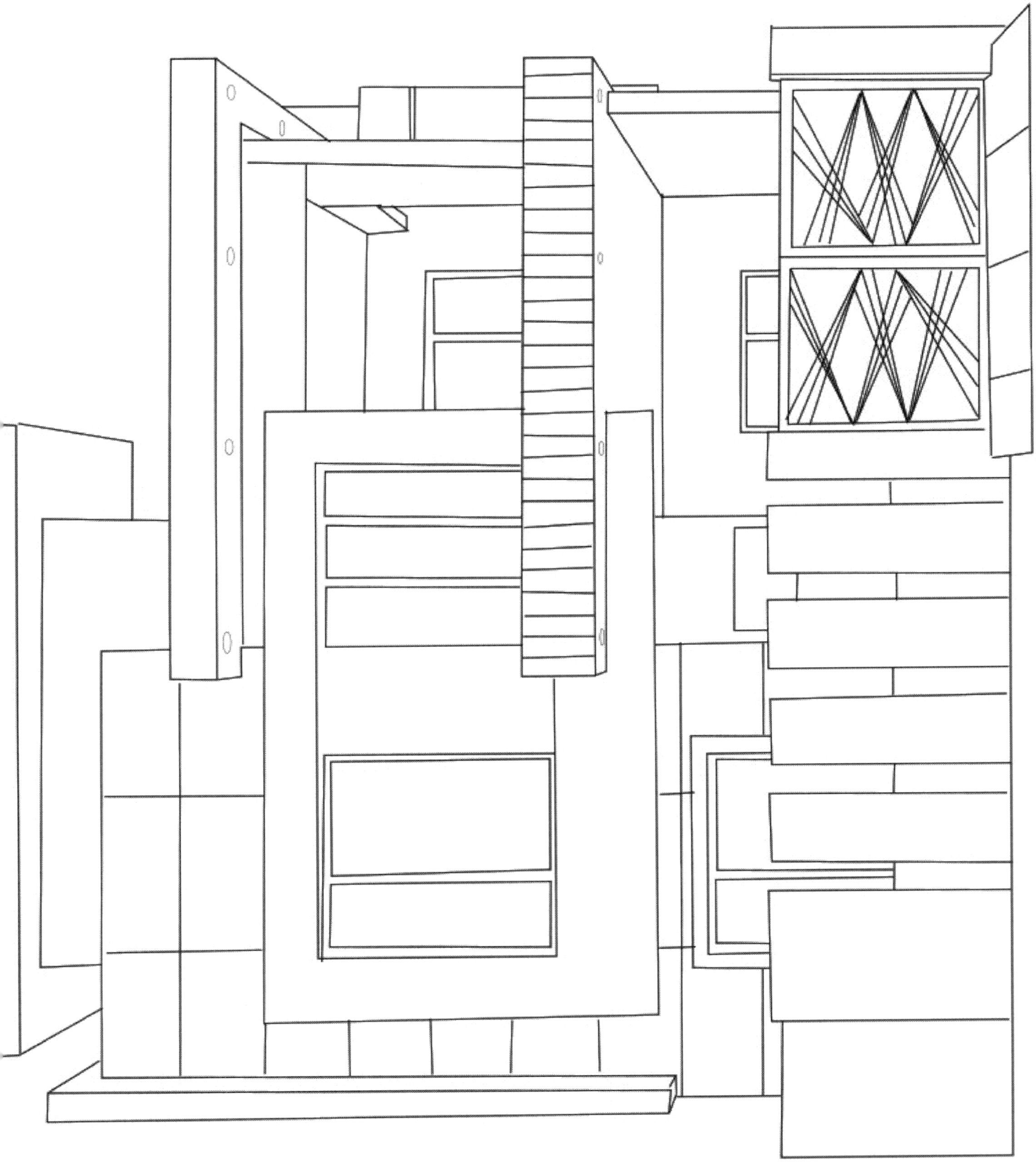

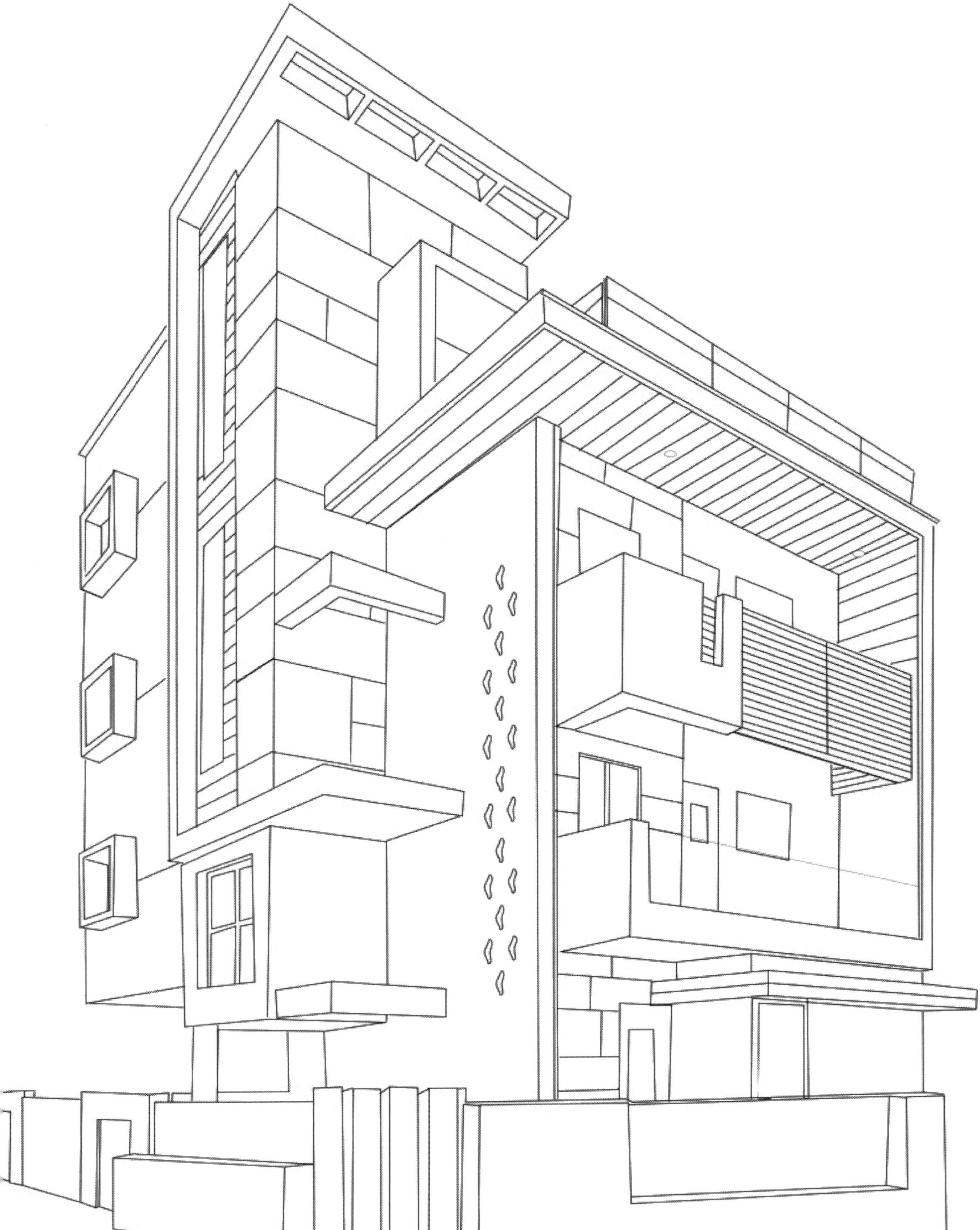

Printed by Amazon Italia Logistica S.r.l.
Torrazza Piemonte (TO), Italy

16095995R00039